The Owl House

A memoir by

Rosemary Gill

The Gill Family

(from left to right) Charles, Brendan, Anne, Michael, Brenda, Holly,

Madelaine, Rosemary, and Kate.

To my darling daughter

Kate Gill Campion

Merci mille fois!

Table of Contents

Foreword

Brendan Gill

Writers directly or indirectly, all poets are teachers; moreover, the greater the poet, the greater the teacher. For me, the greatest poet writing in English in the twentieth century has been Yeats; he is first among my teachers. In one of the most exquisite of his poems-a poem entitled "A Prayer for My Daughter"-Yeats describes pacing up and down beside his daughter Anne's cradle at Thoor Ballylee, hearing the sea wind scream upon the tower and 'imagining in excited reverie that the future years had come.' In the course of this reverie, he draws up a list of the fortunate circumstances he would like her to live among, not least of which is that her bridegroom should "bring her to a house/Where all's accustomed, ceremonious." He then poses a question so profound that at first glance it appears to lack common sense altogether: "How but in custom and in ceremony are innocence and beauty born?"

Puzzling over those words, we are tempted to ask a question or two in return. Surely innocence and beauty must precede custom and ceremony? For are they not among the earliest, most natural, and therefore most uncalculated, of human attributes? And yet little by little we perceive that Yeats has got it right: Innocence and beauty are abstractions, developed at cost over a long period of in the human mind, and the stuff out of which we have created them is learned behavior. We have contrived to stitch together a fabric of agreed-upon rituals and customs, which keep us safe from our primordial, hitherto unpredictable emotions-a fabric composed of a thousand threads, or ten thousand.

Custom and ceremony require not only space, but shelter, as Yeats foresaw in speaking of the house to which he hoped a bridegroom would one day be taking his daughter. There are shelters on every scale, for every purpose. Throughout the centuries, Popes have been crowned in Saint Peter's, that inhumanly vast marble house of God; monarchs equally adept at pomp have met on the Field of the Cloth of Gold, in tents like palaces. In contemporary life we carry out our customs in a more modest fashion, among the informal daily collaborations of private and professional life still; still, our customs are not less precious to us because of how casually we embrace and (often enough) neglect them.

The lares and penates of the ancient Romans were true household gods; guardians of the hearth, who could ward off evil spirits and dangerous situations. Our household gods, in direct descent from these tutelary divinities, are our possessions. They cannot guard us-on the contrary, we have to be continuously guarding *them*-but they provide us with the ever-welcome nourishment of the familiar; they are sacred to us as standing for something stronger and longer lasting than we are. This is especially true of those possessions that, however tarnished with age, and of however little value in themselves, have come down to us out of the past and give us some hint of who we are by reminding us of where we came from. In my family, such possessions would appear to the eye of a stranger to be the merest incoherent jumble of imperfection, odds and ends of furniture, silver, brass, paintings, drawings and the like, and yet to me and my family they are virtually indispensable.

We cherish as household gods a painting that hung long ago in my Grandfather Duffy's library, of Othello telling Desdemona and Brabantio the story of his life ("Her father loved me, oft invited me...."); a nine-foot high case clock in the Gothic style, which, on striking the hour, shakes the whole house; and an early-nineteenth-century walnut table of immense length and breadth, upon whose polished surface some child now long since dead could not resist scratching in an uncertain hand the name "Mama." Is it absurd for me-for all of us- to care so much for what are but objects? Fortunately, my great teacher is eloquent on the subject. He believes in the holiness that objects acquire through age and association. He says we do well to keep them for as long as we can and then face bravely, in whatever generation, the likelihood of their loss. I am content with Yeat's dictum. I glance round from a painted leather fire bucket to a Chelsea cow, to a red-brown ancient edition of *Roderick Hudson*, and gradually I feel good magic stealing into me. They will keep me, those little, disguised gods, safe against the dark.

Architectural Digest 1980

Chapter One
The Owl House

Anne Barnard Gill, radiant, beautiful, brilliant, blond, brown and green-eyed Mother, tosses a bouquet of white roses from the second-floor window of the Lawrence Hospital in Bronxville, New York. The roses tumble down into the arms of Dad, Brendan Michael Gill, brilliant, humorous, black-haired, brown-eyed father and to us, their six children, Brenda, Michael, Holly, Madelaine, Kate and me, Rosemary. We've come to welcome our newborn baby brother, Charles Barnard Gill, and bring him home to The Owl House. In The Owl House Dad says, "The first rule of life is to have a good time. There is no second rule."

We climb into our favorite car, a 1929 maroon Packard touring convertible. Mother and Dad have named the Packard E.Y. for eternal youth. It has jump seats and running boards for children and dogs, and is fitted with a special horn that makes the sound of a cow mooing. Dad in his Brooks brothers tweed jacket, climbs in the driver's seat. Charming black haired Michael (who's nine years old) sits next to him. Adorable, brown haired Kate (she's three) and I (I have brown hair, brown eyes and I'm five) are on the jump seats that have been unfolded from the floor. There's a railing for us to hold. Raven haired beauty Brenda,(she's ten and a half) Curly haired green eyed Holly, (she's eight) and light brown hair deep brown eyed Madelaine, (she's six and a half,) pile into the backseat to sit next to Mother who's holding Charles, (He's one day old) in her arms. As the engine roars to life Dad says, "E.Y. is inherited from the Barnard side of our family, Charles."

Pulling out of the hospital parking lot we drive slowly through traffic, dip beneath an underpass and up onto

Pondfield Road, the main street in the village of Bronxville. One and two story stores line the street. Wide sidewalks with trees on every corner encourage pedestrian traffic. Every block boasts handsome stoplights with buttons placed at child's eye level enabling them to halt cars at will.

Dad shouts over the motor, "Having stoplight buttons at your height children, is the reason we decided to move to Bronxville."

We drive along as fellow villagers stop and wave like spectators at a parade and we wave back wildly. Dad toots the horn. "Moo moo," E.Y. says.

"This is your village, Charles, it's called Bronxville," Madelaine says. We chant, "We're from Bronxville and no one could be prouder, and if you cannot hear us, we'll yell a little louder," repeating a football cheer we've learned at school which goes from kindergarten to twelfth grade. As we drive, we sing. We always sing on car rides-songs like, 'Take me out to the ball game, Take me out to the park' and 'I've been working on the railroad all the livelong day.' While singing I think, I'm very proud to be a Gill.

Now that Charles is born we have seven children in our family, which means the Gill family is the biggest in Lawrence Park. Lots of families have four or five or six children, but we have seven!

I can't wait for Charles to see The Owl House, the most fantastic house in the world. I'll show him the garage with the secret cave and the porch under the porte-cochere with the huge front door. I'll show him the best place to hide in the Front Hall and all the hiding places in the Living Room and the Library and the Gymnasium. Wait till I show Charles the Gym, with the ropes and rings. I'll show him our spooky cellar and Willy's Garden and the Kitchen and the Dining Room and the Landing and then the Whole Upstairs, both floors. I can't wait to show Charles everything in The Owl House. He's going to love it.

We turn off Pondfield Road drive between two stone gateposts and into Lawrence Park. Hundred-year-old oak trees grow in front of magnificent houses built on the rock outcroppings. Streets of yellow and red brick cobblestones wind around sidewalks laid out in herringbone patterns.

Dad brings E.Y. to a slow stop, turns around in his seat "Look at these houses," he says, "They're so joyous and playful; feels good simply to look at them. They don't shut themselves away from the passerby as the brick Georgian and Colonials do. Look at their verandas and bay windows and dormered towers and carved bargeboards and many patterned shingles. Look how they reach out and gather us in and prompt us to share in their manifold felicities. This land belonged to Native Americans two hundred years ago. It was sold it to farmer named Prescott who, in turn, sold it to Mr. Lawrence."

Michael with a big smile says, "We live at 26 Prescott."

Mother says, "I've decided to speak French to our sweet new baby Charles Barnard Gill."

Dad calls out, "Quelle bonne idée!!"

Brenda, showing off her knowledge of French says, "Quelle bonne idée means 'What a good idea' in English, Charles."

Michael, agreeing says, "Vraiment." Brenda says, "Vraiment means 'true' in English, Charles."

Dad starts E.Y. up and drives around the last turn. We spy The Owl House. It rises above pine, magnolia, dogwood, and apple trees to greet us. A large wooden owl is perched on the highest peak of The Owl House's three-peaked roof.

Kate says, "Look, Charles there's our owl on top of the roof."

"Tell Charles about The Owl House Dad," Michael says.

Dad says, "The Owl House is a vast mock Tudor mansion built in 1898, after the style of Henry Hobson Richardson, an architect credited with inspiring America's Romanesque revival. The Owl House is four stories, seventy-nine feet four inches high and thirty-eight feet wide."

"It has twenty-two rooms. I counted them," Holly says. "Eighteen rooms face south. That means they're always filled with sun."

Madelaine climbs from the back seat to the front for a better view and says, "See the chimneys, Charles? They're red brick and they have yellow chimney pots."

Kate exclaims, “You’ll love The Owl house, Charles.”

We chant our traditional family song of praise. “Two, four, six, eight, who do we appreciate?” We sing the first “two, four, six, eight” to Charles with a loud “Hurrah!” Then to Mother and Dad, “Hurrah, Hurrah!” Then Brenda and Michael and Holly, Madelaine, Kate, and me, “Hurrah!” “Hurrah!” “Hurrah!” “Hurrah!” “Hurrah” “Hurrah!”

And finally “Two, four, six, eight, to The Owl House, The Owl House, HURRAH!”

Chapter 2
The Front Hall

Dad blows E.Y.'s horn for a last long moo as we coast through the driveway. We pull past our garage, the first built in Lawrence Park, a twenty- foot high by twenty-foot long stone fort garage with a secret cave. The car comes to a stop under our handsome porte-cochere with a rock wall on one side and a red porch on the other. Everyone climbs out of E.Y. Dad and Michael leap up the six steps of the porch. Michael is wearing blue jeans with the cuffs rolled up, a plaid green shirt and a pair of Keds. "Welcome home Charles. Welcome home to The Owl House," we all shout at once. Charles blinks and coos his delight.

Holly in a dark green cardigan over her light green dress, stands on the porch and waves, "The porch is where we wave and sing farewell to our guests after every party," she says.

Madelaine, smoothes out the ruffles on her checkered blue dress and sings, "Happy trails to you until we meet again..." We all sing, "Keep smiling until then..."

Michael says, "We have guests all the time, Charles. Everyone loves to come to The Owl House."

Kate, in her pink smocked dress, throws her arms up and says, "I love the porch!"

Dad holds the front door open. It's a big heavy door with iron bolts and a giant glass window that gets replaced every Christmas with a 'Grandma Moses style' painting he's done of a snow scene with our family in the country. There's a lovely brass knocker which no one ever uses and a huge doorknob with a big lock. The Owl House is never locked, so we never need keys.

We step over the threshold into the Front Hall. It glows with lights tucked behind elaborate ceiling moldings. The woodwork is painted a soft cream color, which makes the room bright. It smells of wood fires and old books. There are two closets, a door leading to the dining room and a set of stairs going up to a landing. In front of one window next to the front door is a large hour- glass. On the floor is a well-worn Oriental carpet. A tulipwood table holds two silver candlesticks and a letter box from the Civil War with our mail sticking out of it. A large framed mirror hangs on the wall above the table.

We see ourselves reflected in the mirror as Brenda, in a yellow tea dress says, "See the monkeys?" "We do, we do," we shriek making faces and monkey cries at our reflections doubling over in laughter at the old joke.

"I love The Front Hall!" Kate says.

Michael twirls around and says, "Tell Charles more about The Owl House, Dad."

Dad begins, “All the ceilings on the first floor are ten feet tall...” he is interrupted.

“Watch out. Watch out. Here come the animals,”we shout. The Gill family dogs come barking and jumping up on us, they’re so excited to meet Charles.

We have three dogs, a collie named Duffy, two small poodles named Putzel and Jeudi, two cats, one orange colored one named Marmalade, and one white one called Chou-fleur which is French for cauliflower. Two parakeets, named Whistler and Mr. Oiseau, three turtles, a hamster and a guinea pig named Bijou. I think Charles will love playing with the turtles.

“Cut it out,” Dad says to the dogs to stop them from barking but they don’t listen.

Mother, who loves every living thing, reaches down and pets each one, purrs her approval and says, “Bonjour, mes chiens.”

Brenda gives the dogs a kiss and says, “Chien is ‘dog’ in English, Charles.”

“Brenda is a wordsmith,” Dad says proudly.

Mother and Dad believe all of us are geniuses.

Michael pulls open a closet door and shows us the inside stuffed with coats, “The front hall has two coat closets, Charles. This is the best one.” I crawl under the coats (in my smocked pink dress just like Kates) to show Charles how easy it is to disappear and tell him, “This is the best closet for hide and seek. Can you see me? I’m behind the coats.”

Madelaine places her little boots in the other closet and says, “We need to put everything away before our party this afternoon, Charles, it’s a party for you!”

Mother helps Madelaine make space for her boots and says proudly, “Merveilleux, Madelaine.”

Brenda says, “Marveilleux means ‘marvelous’ in English, Charles.”

Michael shuts the closet door and says, “Which room would you like to see next on our Owl House tour, Charles?” Charles thinks.

Holly puts the dogs down, hops under the open doorway from the hall to the living room, and says, "The Living Room should be next on The Owl House tour."

We call out, "The Living Room. The Living Room." Mother waves Charles' baby hand and says, "A bientot, Hall."

Chapter 3

The Living Room

“Two, four, six, eight, who do we appreciate? The Living Room, the Living Room, Hurray!”

We rollick into the sun- filled Living Room.

Kate does somersaults across the Oriental rug and says, “I love the living room.”

Mother gives quick pats and touches to the tops of our heads as we pass by and says, “Le Salon, Charles.”

"Salon means 'living room' in English, Charles," Brenda says.

Michael says, "Tell Charles about the living room Dad."

Dad takes long strides across the room and says, "This room is eighteen feet by thirty-three feet."

Windows on one side of the room overlook the front lawns. On the opposite side they overlook Willy's Garden. Pink, blue, and red flowering plants bloom from window boxes. The windows have red brocade curtains.

I wrap a curtain around me, Madelaine wraps herself in another curtain, "We never close the curtains in the living room," I say, "It takes too long to close them."

Michael picks a red geranium flower from the window box and puts it on top of Charles' blanket. "Look, Charles, here's a flower for you."

Kate lies on the floor points up at the cream colored ceiling with its three beams of dark wood and says, "This is a beamed ceiling."

A 19th-century walnut table eight feet long and four feet wide is on the north side of the room. On its gleaming surface are two impressive blue and red Japanese enamel lamps. Between them is a handsome record player. Piled up on the table are huge coffee table books about art, architecture, and photography. Catalogs from Christies and Sotheby's auction houses are mixed in with current magazines like Life, Look, and The New Yorker, which we call the family weekly because Dad is one of its writers.

"This is called the Sacred Table, Charles," Brenda says, someone very naughty carved 'mama' in it recently."

Kate jumps onto a big red armchair. "I didn't," she says.

Michael stands behind a high-backed, low-seated blue chair across the room. "This is Dad's chair, Charles. He sits and reads in this chair no matter how much noise we make. Dad has great powers of concentration. Are you listening Charles?" he says.

Holly opens the top of a Queen Anne desk and says, "Here's Mother's desk." Mother's desk is like a doll house. It has three tiny staircases leading to a small shelf with four miniature doorways. This is where we keep our precious stationery from Tiffany's in New York City. It's printed, The Owl House, 26 Prescott Avenue, Bronxville, New York and has a drawing by Mother's brother, Uncle Church Barnard, who is an artist. He's drawn the nine members of the Gill family as Owls, from biggest to smallest, sitting on a branch.

Brenda plops on the red couch next to the fireplace, spreads out her petticoats and says, "This is our fireplace, Charles," she says.

A small bottle of Champagne with wine glasses is on top of the low marble table in front of the couch.

Mother picks up a glass, "Let's propose our customary family toast for Charles," she says.

Dad pops the Champagne cork and pours its fizzy bubbles into the glasses, raises his, and cheerfully says, "To ourselves...."

"To each other...." Mother replies.

"To the happiness of us all," we chime in together.

“And to our beloved absent ones,” says Dad, “wherever they may be.”

“Mother, throw your glass into the fireplace, it’s our custom,” Holly insists.

“I love it when Mother throws her glass into the fireplace,” says Kate.

Dad takes Mother’s empty glass and tosses it into the fireplace where it explodes. “That’s for good luck, Charles” he says.

Holly says, “Mother has friends over for tea parties every week and we make Lapsang souchong tea in our big silver tea set right here on the marble table.”

“We make raisin toast with lots of butter to serve with the tea. The toast tastes so delicious,” I say.

“One of Mother’s friends is called Miss Markham. Miss Markham is the principal of the Bronxville Elementary School.” Madelaine says, “Miss Markham likes children better than parents.”

Brenda says with a laugh.

Michael does jumping jacks. "We love Miss Markham," he says breathlessly.

Mother laughs and says, "Naturellement."

Brenda fixes the bow on Madelaine's dress and says, "Naturellment means 'naturally' in English, Charles."

On the mantelpiece are two china Dalton dogs and two ornamental brass candelabras. In the center there's an 18th-century gold clock that never tells the correct time. On the wall above is a framed painting of Little Red Riding Hood holding her basket standing on the step outside the front door of her grandmother's cottage deep in the woods.

"Little Red Riding Hood is a scary story. You'll love it!" Kate says to Charles.

Madelaine points to exquisite hand- painted porcelain ovals glued to the fireplace surround, "Look at these beautiful pictures, Charles," she says," They're pictures of Napoleon's wives. Napoleon was a French emperor," she says.

I start to do jumping jacks and say, "Mother and Dad have lots of cocktail parties in the Living Room, Charles."

"Cocktail parties are parties for grown-ups, Charles."
"Dad tells us to ask guests what they'd like to drink and then he goes into his little bar and makes martinis for them no matter what they say."

Dad sticks his head out of his bar and says, "They never know the difference."

Holly closes the secret drawers in Mother's desk and says to Charles, "By the way, don't ever drink the grown-ups' drinks."

"Why not?" Kate asks as she curls up with Mother and Charles on the green settee.

Brenda answers, "One time little Brendan Behan went around the room and drank all the grown-ups left over drinks and stumbled over to this couch and went sound asleep. He completely missed Sunday lunch," she pats a cushion on the couch next to her, "We hid him under a mink coat."

"At one cocktail party we tied people's ankles to the furniture with yarn. They all kept talking and didn't notice," I say.

Michael plays with the clock on the mantelpiece and says, “Till they started to move and pulled the furniture over.”

“That was so funny,” Kate says.

Dad says, “I don’t like practical jokes. They’re mean-spirited.”

The bar has a wine rack and shelves of liquor bottles next to a very high sink only grown-ups can reach. Above the sink are glasses of all shapes and sizes. Artwork decorates the walls- small paintings and drawings, postcards of Europe, and an eight foot long receipt for groceries is glued to the door jam. A twelve-inch high iron statue of Mercury is cemented on a counter. Mercury was famous in mythology.

“Look Charles, Mercury has wings on his feet and his cap,” Madelaine says, “Robert Graves told us about the gods and goddesses from mythology.”

Dad puts our empty glasses in the bar sink and says, “Robert Graves is the foremost authority on mythology, Charles.”

"Our neighbors were very excited to meet Robert Graves when he came for Sunday lunch," Michael says, "You'll love our neighbors Charles. They have lots of children and we get to walk to school with them up and down the yellow brick hill.

Madelaine and I turn the record player on and the sound of trumpets from Verdi's Aida fill the room.

"The Gill family loves operas, Charles," Michael says, "And Broadway Musicals. Peter Pan, Oklahoma, South Pacific, Brigadoon...."

I open the record closet on the far wall, "Here's our special closet for records," I say.

Brenda giggles and says, "If a record skips, Dad takes it off the turntable and breaks it in half and sometimes he throws it across the room."

"Yes that's true. It's infuriating to hear a scratched record. I can't stand the skipping," Dad says.

We skip around the living room to Aida.

Mother says, "Quelle noisettes."

Brenda says, "Quelle noisette is 'what nuts' in English, Charles."

Holly says, "Let's continue The Owl House tour. Let's show Charles the Library."

"A bientot Living Room," says Mother.

Brenda says, "A bientot," means 'see you later' in English, Charles."

Kate skips out of the Living Room, "A bientot Living Room," she says.

Chapter 4

The Library

"Two, four, six, eight, who do we appreciate? The Library, the Library, Hurray!"

We march through the double doors into the blissful Library. There are two- story high leaded windows on one wall and two large windows on the other. All the windows have window seats upholstered in green and gold fabric with curtains to match. Built in bookshelves line the walls. Above a twenty-two foot high stone fireplace is a ladder that runs along a serpentine rail that we can climb to reach every book.

Mother inhales the delicious smell of books and says to Charles, "La Bibliotheque."

"La Bibliotheque is 'the Library', in English, Charles," Brenda says.

Kate climbs on a window seat, "I love the Library!" she says.

Michael says, "Tell us about The Owl House Library, Dad."

Dad takes a book down from a shelf, "The Library is twenty feet by eighty feet and two stories high. Oh, Bravo!" He says, here's the Henry James I've been looking for."

Michael plays the Steinway grand piano. "This is Mozart Charles I'll teach you how to play Mozart one day, look Mother Charles is listening," he says.

Kate begs, "Teach me! Teach me! Teach me how to play Mozart."

Michael plays "Twinkle little star" and we all sing along.

A ten by fifteen-foot Gill family portrait by artist Nancy Ellen Craig hangs on the wall behind the piano.

Mother gazes at the portrait, "Nancy Ellen Craig studied at the Academie Julian in Paris."

Madelaine, sniffing the portrait says, "I love the smell of oil paint." "Tell Charles about the portrait Dad."

"Madelaine is the family artist, Charles," Dad says, "Almost fifty years ago, long before any of you were born, William T. Smedley, who owned The Owl house before us, whose pictures we still find in the attics, used this library for his studio. Smedley was a highly successful portrait painter and illustrator who vied with John Singer Sergeant for commissions."

Michael stands up, strikes a chord on the piano and asks, "John Singer Sergeant?"

Brenda on the fire fender tosses her hair and says teasingly, "The John Singer Sargent?"

Holly fixes Charles' blanket and says, "John Singer Sargent was a famous portrait painter."

Dad pushes the big ladder along the rail and says, "When Nancy Ellen Craig became our neighbor, your mother and I commissioned her to paint our family portrait right here in the Library."

Michael studies the portrait and says, "I'm sorry you're not in the portrait Charles."

"We'll have you painted in," Dad says as he gives Charles a kiss.

We hop back and forth over Oriental rugs from window seat to window seat. We pretend the floor is the ocean and there are sharks.

I say, "The Library is a great room for games like Touch my hand before I die, or Blind man's bluff."

In the middle of the Library, Holly puts her hands over her head and says, "This is where the Christmas tree goes." "Our Christmas tree is fifteen feet tall."

Michael pumps his fist in the air "Charles, you're going to love Christmas," he says.

We skip about and sing, "We wish you a Merry Christmas, We wish you a Merry Christmas and a happy New Year."

I can't wait for Charles' first Christmas in The Owl House. It's so exciting. First we run up and down the hall shouting "Wake up, wake up! It's Christmas!" Mother and Dad lead us downstairs to the closed Library doors which he throws open to reveal Santa has come. Our Christmas tree is decorated with hundreds of lights and thousands of shiny bulbs and surrounded by stacks of presents taller than any of us. Charles will be amazed.

"Santa brings millions of presents, Charles," Kate says, "Last Christmas Santa brought me a blow up Bozo clown. He has sand in his feet so when you hit him he bounces back up and you can hit him again. I'll let you try it, Charles."

Mother gives Kate a kiss and says, "What a darling child you are, Kate Bowen."

Inside the small bathroom Brenda says, "Here's the bathroom, Charles."

The walls of the bathroom are hung with framed cartoons drawn by Dad's co-workers and friends, Charles Addams, Saul Steinberg and William Steig.

"These are called cartoons, but they are great art," Dad tells us.

Madelaine touches the canvas of an oil painting of a half naked woman holding her hair over her head. Next to the figure there's a heart with initials A.B.G. and B.G inside it. "This is a Smedley painting, but Dad painted the heart," she says.

Michael lies on the floor and moves his hands and feet like scissors to catch anyone who dares come near. We love this dangerous game.

Dad says, "Roughhousing belongs in the Gym, children."

Holly says, "The Gym is the next room on the tour, Charles."

Mother says, "A bientot Bibliotechique,"

Kate says, "A bientot Library."

Chapter 5

The Gymnasium

“Two, four, six, eight, who do we appreciate? The Gym, the Gym, Hurray!”

Dad opens the heavy soundproof door from the Library to the Gym. We rush past him into the vast Gymnasium. It is two stories high. There are skylights on three roofs and two musicians’ balconies. Screwed into the wall next to one balcony is a sturdy varnished ladder that runs floor to ceiling. Another ladder, just as tall as the first, can be lowered and raised on a pulley manned by children. The ladders make platforms for monkey bars, high -wire acts, rope swings, ring tricks, and a barre for ballet lessons. A climbing rope three inches thick hangs down from the forty-seven- foot tall ceiling. Two leather-covered rings hang four feet from the floor. A basketball net is on one side of the room with a basketball court painted on the surface of the highly varnished wood floor. A wall of wooden lockers leads to an alcove with a small stage and a proscenium declaring it *Le Theatre du Hibou.* On the south wall five windows lead to a roof full of skylights. An outside door has a small porch with stairs leading to the driveway.

Kate runs towards a tricycle under one of the balconies and says, “I love the Gym.”

Mother twirls around and says, “Le Gymnasium.”

Brenda says, “Le Gymnasium is ‘gymnasium’ in English, Charles.”

Michael hangs from a ladder and says, “Tell us about the Gym, Dad.”

Dad looks up at the ceiling and takes long strides across the room, “The Gym is twenty-five feet wide by sixty feet long and two stories high. Smedley built this room as his second studio and took great care to insure it ran right up against his property line. When Mother and I purchased The Owl House in 1947, the Bronxville School was building its gymnasium so we were able to have the same contractors install ours."

Brenda reaches up to hang from the rings. "These are our rings. You can do lots of tricks on them," she says.

Kate swats the rope and says, "You can ride on this big rope when you get older, Charles."

Michael climbs the ladder with rope in hand saying, "Look, I'll show you how to ride the rope, Charles. You need to pull it over to the ladder and jump on it like this," he takes off.

Holly watches Michael jump onto the big knot on the rope and swing past her as she says, "You have to be able to hold on and jump Charles."

Dad opens and closes the doors in the row of wooden lockers and says, "Watch out for the rest of us boy."

"Listen Charles," I say seriously, "Don't ever pull the rope up to the balcony and sit on the end of it and jump because the rope will try to snap you off and smash you through that skylight and that might be the end of you."

Kate rides her tricycle furiously around the room shouting, "Rosemary is accident prone."

Madelaine and I climb on the stage, "Dad built this stage. He made the *Theatre du Hibou* sign, too. See? He used glass doorknobs to make the owl's eyes. They light up in the dark," I say.

Madelaine practices curtsies in front of a backdrop painted with a scene of the streets of Paris- a scene of the city with its century- old houses complete with dormer windows, tile roofs and Vive de Gaulle graffiti. Madelaine points to the backdrop and says, "Here's the Eiffel Tower, Charles. The Eiffel tower is in Paris, France."

Kate climbs on the stage to have a closer look. She says, "Dad painted Paris with glow-in-the-dark paint."

Michael turns on the stage black light. Everything white turns black and Paris becomes the City of Lights.

Mother waltzes in front of the stage and says,"Le Theatre du Hibou."

Brenda says, "Hibou is 'owl' in English, Charles." Dad built the stage for one of our parties."

Dad pulls thick exercise mats out from under the stage and says, "Jane Austen said, 'everything important happens at parties.'"

Michael, swinging on the rope says, "The Gym is the perfect place for parties, Charles." "It gets decorated with balloons and streamers and Japanese lanterns and millions of candles for parties."

Mother sings, "I could have danced all night... I could have danced all night, and still have begged for more." Dad takes Mother and Charles in his arms waltzing and singing, "I could have spread my wings and done a thousand things I'd never done before...". We find partners and dance about the Gym singing, "We could have danced danced danced all night."

Brenda lets go of Holly's hands and says, "Let's sing Three Jolly Coachmen."

"Ooh, la la," says Mother laughing.

"One two, and three jolly coachmen sat in an English tavern..." Dad sings as we all burst out laughing and sing together.

I climb the ladder next to the balcony outside my bedroom.

Madelaine holds another ladder and puts her little feet into first position, then second position. "Mrs. Kelsey gives ballet lessons in the Gym every week," she says.

Michael leaps across Kate's abandoned tricycle and says, "Ballet is only for girls, Charles."

"Some of the greatest ballet dancers in the world are men." Dad replies.

Brenda pushes the tricycle to a safe space. "This is where Mother has her Sunday-school play rehearsals," she says, "Mother teaches Sunday school, Dad is a collapsed Catholic."

In front of a six-foot high replica of Noah's Ark with gangplank Holly says, "Look, Charles, this is Noah's Ark. Dad made it."

Outside on the small porch Kate says, "See Charles? Here's the way out."

Dad gestures Kate inside and says," Time for The Owl House tour to continue."

"The Cellar is next," says Holly.

Dad says, "Good idea I need to check the furnace."

Mother says, "La Cave."

Brenda says, "La Cave is 'the cellar' in English, Charles."

Michael lifts up a trapdoor under the stage. "This way to the Cellar ladies and gentlemen," he announces.

Dad leads the way and waits for us at the bottom of a set of steep stairs.

Kate blows a kiss behind her, "A bientot Gym," she says.

Chapter 6

The Cellar

"Two, four, six, eight, who do we appreciate? The Cellar, the Cellar Hurray!"

"Go down the stairs one at a time," Brenda says, "Be careful. Take your time."

Dad says, "The ceilings in the Cellar are eight feet high."

We shout, "Eight feet high!" as we pass him on the last step.

The Cellar has six big rooms. Below the Gym is the second artist studio with a five paned skylight and a door that leads to Willy's Garden. Another door goes to a room that has a row of small windows high on one wall. The next room has a small-enclosed toilet, a boiler, and The Owl House furnace and another door leading to Willy's Garden. There's a shelved pantry room and a laundry room with floor to ceiling windows and two large sinks. Beside it is a rectangular room with windows facing the driveway and a set of stairs that lead up to the kitchen. Another door leads into a square room with three big ground floor windows and a deep farmer's sink overlooking the oak tree terrace in Willy's garden.

Kate hugs Mother's legs and says, "I love the Cellar."

"The Cellar is built over huge boulders which make theoutside wall over a foot-and-a-half thick," Dad says.

Michael slaps the boulders with his hands and says, "The walls protect The Owl House in cold weather."

Madelaine holds Holly's hand tightly and says, "The Cellar is kind of spooky, Charles." Charles blinks in the dark.

We climb down three stone steps into the second artist's studio and pass through a stone entrance into a dimly lit room. There's an old turquoise couch, a round birch table with four chairs, and a walnut bar with matching stools. There's a T.V. where we get to watch Leonard Bernstein's children's concerts. The walls are painted purple.

"This room is my clubhouse," Michael says. "It's called the Purple Palace, Charles." "When I get my driver's license, Dad said I can drive E.Y. My friends and I are going to dress up like gangsters and come back to the Purple Palace to celebrate our misdeeds," Michael says.

"Peut-etre," Mother says to Michael.

Brenda says, "Peut-etre means 'maybe' in English, Charles."

We follow each other and step down into a large rectangular room where we crouch down with Dad as he makes his inspection of the furnace.

Dad finishes tinkering, gets up, and says, "All's well with the furnace."

Mother tests the dryness of clothes hanging from a clothesline that stretches across the room and says, “Bravo, furnace!”

Holly calls from the next room, “Who wants a popsicle?” she asks.

There’s a big freezer against a wall of the room, which is fifteen feet long and ten feet wide with stairs that go up to the kitchen.

I help Holly lift the lid of the freezer and say, “This is our freezer, Charles. We hide popsicles below the frozen vegetables, so there’s always one waiting for us.” We hand out the popsicles.

Kate licks her popsicle and goes into the next room, “See Charles, the Owl House has two kitchens,” she says. Dad says, “This room is the original kitchen for The Owl house.”

The floor is tiled. On one wall there’s a large framed photograph of Mother and Dad on their wedding day.

Michael, standing below the photo, says, “Tell Charles how you met Mother, Dad.”

Dad looks at the photograph and says, “Your Mother and I met because roommates of mine at Yale had crushes on Anne Barnard, a student at Smith College. They drove from New Haven to Northampton every weekend to try to persuade her to go out with them. As a prank, they bet her that she wouldn’t have the courage to write a letter to their shy bookworm friend, me.”

Mother with a radiant smile says, “I’d never known anyone named Brendan, and I loved the idea of a bookworm. Your father wrote an exquisite letter back to me.”

“I thought Anne Barnard was a beautiful name from the first moment I heard it,” Dad says, smiling back at her.

“Oh, Dad” we all say. Charles coos.

“Grandpro said; “Nothing could make my daughter, Anne, happier than to be married to a writer.” Dad says.

Holly says, “Granpro is Mother’s father, Charles. He lives in Asheville, North Carolina.”

Brenda fixes my ponytail and says, " Gramere (Mother's mother) had a dress shop in Asheville. Guess who came in every day to visit her, Charles."

Michael digs through a barrel of clay and says, "I guess F. Scott Fitzgerald!"

Dad nods yes and says, "That's right. F. Scott Fitzgerald's wife, Zelda, was in a sanitarium in Asheville. After Scott visited her there he would come by Gramere's dress shop and sit on the chaise lounge in the front window and they talked for hours."

"F. Scott Fitzgerald is a great writer," says Holly.

Michael laughs and says, "That's why he called his book The GREAT Gatsby!" "Tell Charles what John O'Hara said about Mother, Dad."

"John O'Hara is another great writer, Charles," says Holly.

Dad says, "John spoke with tremendous enthusiasm about Mother. He said how pretty and alive she is, and how impressed he was by her intelligence. Also her loved her voice and he wondered how I could be away from her and I admitted it was pretty hard."

We throw our popsicle sticks into the huge wastebasket under the sink and Dad says, "Your other Grandfather, Grandpa Gill, who lived in Hartford, CT. knew Samuel Clemens, another great writer, whose pen name was Mark Twain. Grandpa Gill once saw Mr. Clemens walk down the street to the liquor store in his bathrobe and slippers in the middle of a snow storm."

Madelaine sits in one of the six wooden chairs at a large pine table in the middle of the room and arranges crayons by color. "Our friends love to do art here," she says.

I bring Charles an old candle I've found by the sink and say, "For Thanksgiving, we make candles by dipping wicks into melted wax. See the old wax on the table?" I say.

Dad sings the well known Thanksgiving hymn, "We gather together to ask the Lord's blessing..." We join in adding descants.

"This is the dumb-waiter, Charles. We use it to send things upstairs," Brenda says as she opens the dumbwaiter door and pulls on the ropes inside.

"This is Dad's wine cellar," Madelaine says from a closet stacked floor to ceiling with bottles packed in straw.

In the tiled- front hall of the old kitchen, Holly pulls on the heavy wooden door to Willy's Garden trying to open it. "Help," she says, "It's time for a tour of Willy's Garden." Dad tugs the door open and says, "Next stop on The Owl House tour, Willy's Garden."

Kate rubs a small ball of clay in her hands, tosses it on the table and says, "A bientot cellar."

Chapter 7

Willy's Garden

"Two, four, six, eight, who do we appreciate? Willy's Garden, Willy's Garden, Hurray!"

Michael first out the door says, "Tell us about Willy's Garden, Dad."

Dad pushes the heavy door to the Cellar shut and says, "Willy's Garden is carved out of the same rock The Owl House sits on. Willy was a gardener your Mother and I met when we bought The Owl House. Although we had a limited budget, creative Willy filled our Garden with extraordinary trees, bushes and flowers. It became evident during neighbors' visits that Willy was removing shrubbery from their yards and planting them in ours. Not the right thing to do, of course, but we all considered him a beloved rascal."

"I love Willy's garden!" says Kate.

Willy's Garden has paths that lead from The Owl House to Look Out Avenue to Park Avenue which we call the yellow brick hill that leads to the village center and The Bronxville School. The school band on the football field far below is playing the school anthem, "Here's to Bronxville, our alma mater, we hail the gray and blue." We proudly sing along.

On the a terrace bordered by a twelve-foot high stonewall on one side, and a rock with deep cervices on the other, Michael hops from slate tile to slate tile. "If ever you walk in a London street, be ever so careful to watch your feet, and keep in the squares or the masses of bears, all ready to eat...." he says laughing.

Kate hops behind him and says, "Stop, Michael, you're scaring me!"

Madelaine, from atop the rock pools says, "A.A. Milne is not a scary poet."

"This is Desema, Charles," Brenda says as she pats an eighteen-inch- high bronze sculpture of a girl holding an urn. Holly reaches under a step below Brenda's feet to turn on a faucet that makes water pour out of the urn and run into the pools.

"I love Willy's Garden," Kate says.

"We put goldfish in the pools one time, but the cats ate them," Michael says with a wicked grin.

"Pauvre poisson," Mother says.

"Pauvre poisson means 'poor fish' in English, Charles," Brenda says.

"One man's fish is another man's poisson," Dad says as a joke.

"Mother had a treasure hunt for us in Willy's garden, With you as the treasure Charles," Holly says.

"We had to answer five riddles," Michael says as we run down a path between a stand of pine trees and the high wall of the oak tree terrace to our swing set playground. "The first riddle was 'What squeaks and swings'?"

We swing on the swings and slide down the slide. Kate says, "What was the next riddle?"

We run up the path from the swing set past the old stone porch of The Owl House next to the tall windows of the laundry room of the Cellar and stop at the hundred foot high oak tree planted in the center of a slate terrace with six-foot high apple trees growing in each corner. "The second riddle was 'from what mighty trees do acorns grow?'" Holly says.

Mother sits with Charles on one of the three trunks of the oak tree, looks up at the branches and says, "L'arbre magnifique."

Brenda sits on another trunk and says, "L'arbre magnifique means 'magnificent tree' in English, Charles."

Madelaine picking up acorn tops says, "The third riddle...?"

Michael, in the branches above Mother's head says, "The riddle was 'Still waters run deep.' Come on, I'll show you the answer," he says as he jumps down.

We run down another path to a deep rock pool shielded from the road by three tall pine trees. The pool is deep enough to submerge in water up to our necks.

Kate, disappointed that the pool has only just begun to fill with water, says, “The riddle was floating on top.”

Michael says, “This is where we found the final answer to our treasure hunt, Charles,” he says. Charles gurgles.

Dad kisses Charles on the head, and says, “The Treasure we found at the end of the riddle was you my boy,” he says.

Mother says, “Mon tresor.”

Brenda kisses Charles and says, “Tresor is a ‘treasure’ in English, Charles.”

“Treasure doesn't always mean money, Charles,” Michael says.

“Treasures! Treasures! We’re all treasures,” we sing.

“Oh, we ain’t got a barrel of money, maybe we’re ragged and funny, but we’ll travel along, singing a song, side by side.”

Holly says, “It’s time for The Owl House tour to go on. Let’s show Charles the kitchen.”

Mother says, “Avanti, La Cuisine.”

Brenda says, “La Cuisine is ‘The Kitchen’ in English, Charles.”

Madelaine says, “A bientot Jardin de Willy.”

Kate, with a big wave says, “A bientot Willy’s Garden.”

Chapter 8
The Kitchen

“Two, four, six, eight, who do we appreciate? The Kitchen, the Kitchen, Hurrah!”

We climb a set of twelve small slate steps up to the kitchen terrace at the top of the garage parapet and to the kitchen door.

Dad holds the door open, “Come one, come all for a tour of The Owl House Kitchen,” he says.

The kitchen is warm and cozy. It smells of butter. There’s a double window over a sink across from the stove. Mother puts Charles in Dad’s arms and goes to the sink to fill a big glass with water and drinks it.

Dad with a grimace says, “I don’t like holding babies, even my own, I’m afraid their heads will roll off.” We laugh as Brenda and Holly give us little cups of water. Mother retrieves Charles from Dad and gives him her refilled water glass to drink.

“Here’s the stove, Charles. Be careful. It’s hot! There’s always something cooking on it,” Madelaine says. “Mother’s beef stew is famous.”

“So is Dad’s Bourbon meatloaf,” says Holly.

Mother puts a big bowl of grapes on the table near the dumbwaiter and says, “Mache bien avec vos dents.”

“Maché bien avec vos dents means ‘Chew well with your teeth’ in English, Charles,” Brenda says.

I pick a few grapes from the bowl and count them out on the table, "Charles doesn't have any teeth yet," I say.

Kate with a mouthful of grapes says, "I love the Kitchen!"

Michael opens the icebox door across from two staircases that lead to the cellar and the landing and says, "Here's our ice box, Charles." He shows Charles a bottle of ketchup and a stick of butter, "These are my two favorite things. You'll love them, too." he says.

Dad, from the pantry says, "Michael puts ketchup on everything."

Kate, next to the sink, stares at a two layer yellow cake with chocolate frosting and says, "This is our cake. We have cake every day for our after school treats," she says.

Madelaine makes a funny face and says in a conspiratorial whisper, "Mother pours wine on her cake."

Mother with a blissful smile says, " Oui, C'est delicieux."

Brenda says, "Delicieux means 'delicious' in English, Charles."

Holly says, "Here's the dumb-waiter again, Charles. These are the shelves we put things on to send them up to the nursery or down to the Cellar."

"Let's play in the dumb waiter," Kate says.

Mother says, "Oh please don't play in there. Jamais!"

Brenda says, "Jamais means 'never' in English, Charles."

Taking a handful of grapes Dad says, "The dumbwaiter is not for playing in."

There's a butler's pantry with shelves and a sink. Gold-rimmed serving dishes, plates with hand painted flowers and fruit, glass plates etched with sparkling designs.

"These are some of the beautiful dishes from our ancestors. Ancestors are family, Charles," Madelaine says. Charles burps.

The butler's pantry is adjacent to the breakfast room which has a high ceiling and a wall of windows overlooking the oak tree terrace in Willy's Garden. There's a Formica table with a bench large enough to seat five built against the wall on one side, and another desk for Mother.

"The breakfast room is where we have supper every night, peanut butter and jelly sandwiches and tomato soup," I say.

"We have our dinner in the middle of the day."

"People in Europe eat dinner in the middle of the day, too," Holly says.

"The kitchen is always full of treats and people, especially during parties," I say as I rummage through the photos on Mother's desk.

Michael throws grapes in the air and catches them in his mouth. "The Gills love parties," he says.

Kate says, "We are a party."

Brenda eats her grapes from a stem she's holding and says, "Parties mean we'll be washing dishes, all our fancy dishes, and glasses, hundreds of glasses."

Michael says, "We had a dishwasher once, but it broke."

Madelaine climbs a chair to reach more grapes, "Don't worry, Charles, boys don't do dishes," she says.

Dad washes the water glasses and says, “I do dishes.”

We all sing, “Someone’s in the kitchen with Dinah, someone’s in the kitchen I know...”

“Let’s go to the Dining Room next,” says Holly.

Dad pushes open the door to the Dining Room and announces, “The Owl House tour of the Dining Room.”

Mother says, “ Ah oui, La Salle a Manger.”

Brenda says, “La Salle a Manger means ‘dining room’ in English, Charles.”

Kate runs her little finger over the icing at the bottom of the cake, licks it, and says, “A bientot Kitchen.”

Chapter 9

The Dining Room

“Two, four, six, eight, who do we appreciate? The Dining Room, the Dining Room, Hurray!”

The oval Dining Room has architectural murals on the walls above four-foot high wainscoting. A cherry wood dining table with eight matching chairs is the centerpiece of the room. A walnut buffet table against one wall sits opposite eight windows with floor length golden curtains. White Victorian birdcages hang over a window box filled with flowering plants and small statues of lions and owls made of brass and iron and random curiosities, a piece of pink coral that looks like a brain and chunks of petrified wood which peek out between the flowers.

Madelaine, at the windows says, “See our birds, Charles? This one is named Pete, and this one is named Oiseau.”

Mother whistles hello to the birds and checks their food and water. Sometimes she opens the doors on their cages to let them fly about the room. Mother reminds me of Snow White.

Michael says, “Tell Charles about The Owl House Dining Room, Dad.”

Dad inspects a large aquarium filled with tropical fish near the Kitchen door and says, “The Dining Room is fourteen feet by twenty-four feet.”

Holly helps herself to a few M&M’s from the candy dish in the center of the table and says, “Oval dining rooms are very rare.”

We follow Holly's example and take some M&M's from the dish. The Gills are famous for serving M&M's on every occasion.

Kate shows us how to balance the candy on her tongue and says, "I love the Dining Room!"

Dad admires a mural and says, "These are valuable murals of the four famous squares in Paris."

Brenda sits at the table with Kate on her lap, "Paris is where they speak French just like we do, Charles," she says.

Michael, with his mouth full of candy says, "Look at the ceiling. The Dining Room ceiling is decorated with streamers and balloons, some old, some new. People always look up at the Dining Room ceiling to see the decorations."

Madelaine puts M&M's on the table according to color and says, "We have birthdays here all year long. Today the decorations are for you, Charles, to celebrate your birthday."

We sing "Happy Birthday to you, Happy Birthday to you." Charles snuffles.

Built into the wall next to the pocket doors leading to the living room is a glass-fronted china cabinet filled with demitasse cups and saucers.

Holly holds a conch shell from the window box up to her ear to hear the ocean and says, "We have our special Sunday lunches in the Dining Room. Millions of friends come to Sunday lunch. Sometimes children get to sit at a special table just for them," she says.

Michael says, "We sing the Doxology at Sunday lunch. I'll teach you how to sing it, Charles." 'Praise God from whom all blessings flow, Praise him all creatures here below...'

"During lunch it's fun to play games with our guests, Charles. One game is passing things like salt and pepper and butter around and around the table while the guests are busy talking, and we all have a big laugh when they catch on," I say.

Dad reaches for an M&M and says, "You mustn't do that."

Madelaine licks chocolate from her finger and says, "We like to recite poems for them. Poems from the Victorian age when a lot of children died."

With a red a green and a brown M&M in my mouth I say, "And Robert Frost poems, and poems by Walt Whitman, and Browning and Rossetti, and Dylan Thomas."

Mother shows Charles the china cabinet and says, "Ah oui, s'il vous plait reciter un maintenant."

Brenda says, "S'il vous plait reciter un maintenant means 'oh please recite one now' in English, Charles."

We recite the Victorian one, "The little toy dog is covered in dust, but sturdy and staunch he stands. The little toy soldier is red with rust and his musket moulds in his hands. Time was when the little toy dog was new and the soldier was passing fair, and that was the time when our Little Boy Blue Kissed them and put them there..."

Dad adjusts the lampshades on the light scones and interrupts us saying, "Heartbreaking, Heartbreaking."

We love poetry. It's the custom at Sunday Lunch during dessert for Dad to read poetry at the table. For us and all our guests. Usually the poems of his favorite poet, Yeats. He uses a special poet voice, "We can dance, we can sing, we are blessed by everything and everything we look upon is blest," Dad says.

Kate climbs on a high chair and says, "I'm a poet."

Michael jokes, "I'm a poet, but I don't know it, but my feet show it. They're Longfellow's." We all laugh.

Mother sits at the head of the table with Charles in her lap as she brushes kates' hair back in place, "The marvelous poet Marianne Moore came to Sunday lunch," she says.

Dad tinkers with the valve on the radiator and says, "Marianne Moore said, 'The Gill family has an insatiable appetite for life.' I like that."

"Exactement, ma famille," Mother says with delight,

Brenda says, "Exactement ma famille is 'exactly, my family' in English, Charles."

The Poet Wallace Stevens wrote 'The words of the world are the life of the world.' Wallace Stevens is from Hartford," Dad says proudly.

"Dad is from Hartford, Charles," Michael says.

Across the room Holly says, "Mother is from the Mayflower."

Brenda fixes the candles in the candlesticks on the table and says, "On school days we eat breakfast and lunch in the Dining Room."

Madelaine says, "We come home from school for lunch, Charles. One of my friends who came to lunch said she'd never eaten creamed hot dogs before."

Underneath the dining room table is a button that buzzes in the kitchen to let the servants know it's time to clear the table. We don't have any servants. I press the button and we hear several short buzzes, "Listen, Charles, that's our secret buzzer," I say.

The mahogany sideboard with lion's head brass fittings on each of its drawers sits across from the windows. On top of it is a grand silver tea set between two Chinese vases. A gold-framed painting of Othello hangs on the wall.

"Tell Charles about the time all our silver was stolen, Dad," Michael says.

Dad inspects his carving knives inside the sideboard and says, "One day, when I was at work in the city, a gentleman came to The Owl House and told Mother he was sent to take an inventory of our silver for the insurance company."

Mother says, "He said he was from the insurance company. He looked like a very nice man. He sat at the dining room table all day examining everything and writing notes."

Brenda says, "I remember that man, I made him tea."

"By the time he left, he had stolen all our most valuable pieces, putting them in suitcases he'd brought with him.

We didn't discover the loss till months afterwards," Dad says shaking his head.

Mother says, "Il est tres mechant!"

Brenda says, “Il est tres mechant means ‘very naughty’ in English, Charles.”

Dad flicks the lights from the brass sconces on and off the way they do at theater intermissions.

“Got no diamonds, got no pearls...” we sing.

Holly says, “The Landing is next on the tour. Let’s go to The Owl House Landing.”

Mother gives Holly a kiss and says, “Alors, allons-y la chamber-voisine.”

Brenda says,“ Alors, allons-y la chamber-voisine means ‘let’s go to the next room’ in English, Charles.”

Kate grabs a last handful of M&M’s. “A bientot Dining Room,” she says.

Chapter 10

The Landing

"Two, four, six, eight, who do we appreciate? The Landing, the Landing, Hurray!"

We go through the dining room door into the front hall and up a six-step staircase bordered by fluted columns and an archway with brackets of angels.

Madelaine, under the arches says, “Look at the angels, Charles.” Charles blinks.

Michael rings a set of Tibetan gongs that hang on the side of the stairs. “We ring these bells to announce Sunday lunch, Charles,” he says.

The Landing has a window seat running under two-story leaded bay windows. There are long chintz curtains that have drawings of castles and knights on them. Holly and Madelaine lift up the top of the window seat.

Holly says, “Look, Charles, this window seat is a good place to hide.” They climb inside to prove it.

Kate says, “I love the Landing!”

Standing at the foot of the stairs leading to the second floor I say, “Here’s our grandfather clock, you can hide next to it.” I squeeze in next to the clock.

Kate says, “Hear the chimes, Charles? The grandfather clock’s chiming right now.”

Dad, winding the clock, says, “When it strikes the hour it shakes the whole house.”

Mother looks around and says, "Ou est ma camera? Je voudrais de photographier my belle famille."

Brenda says, "Je voudrais de photographier ma belle famille means 'I want to take a picture of my beautiful family' in English, Charles."

Michael runs down the kitchen stairs to get mother's camera from her desk in the breakfast room. He finds it hidden behind stacks of books by Dante, our drawings, and piles of photographs. "Here it is! Voila!" he shouts, and with an exaggerated bow hands Mother her Kodak camera.

Mother puts Charles carefully in Holly's arms and says, "O Glorioso!"

Holly is on the window seat between Madelaine and me. Kate, Brenda and Michael join us. Dad sits down next to Holly and says, "Be quick, Andy Pandy, we have the rest of The Owl House tour to go."

Dad calls mother Andy Pandy. Mother calls him Brendan Michael.

Mother holds her camera up finds us in the sight. “Everyone say ‘je t’aime’,” she says.

Brenda says, “Je t’aime means ‘I love you’ in English, Charles.”

“Je t’aime! Je t’aime! We all say. Mother snaps the photo.

“It’s time for The Owl House tour of the upstairs,” Holly says as she puts Charles back into Mother’s arms.

Kate climbs down from the window seat and says, “A bientot Landing.”

Chapter 11

Third Floor

“Two, four, six, eight, who do we appreciate? The Third Floor, the Third Floor, Hurray!”

Dad and Brenda lead the way up the stairs past the grandfather clock chiming again, and past the Currier and Ives prints hanging on the wall. Michael and Holly hold the banister as they climb the stairs backwards. Kate, Mother and I follow them singing, “There’s a long, long trail a-winding to the land of our dreams...”

Michael says, “It’s a long climb, Charles.”

Holly opens the door at the top of the stairs, "We're going to the Third Floor first," she says.

We climb the steep staircase up to the Third Floor.

Dad says, "This is the top of The Owl House, over eighty feet high."

The Third Floor rooms are beneath the highest eaves of The Owl House. Three large bedrooms off a shared hall have window views through treetops on both sides of the house. There's a small bathroom with a skylight over its tub.

I open a small frosted glass door at the top of the stairs and say, "Here's the bathroom."

Madelaine holds the rim of a small sink and says, "This is a marble pedestal sink."

Kate tries to get in the bathtub and says, "This is a claw foot tub."

Dad runs his fingers over the edge of the skylight above the sink and says, "This skylight is over a century old. People say they don't build things the way they used to, but the truth is everything built badly fell down."

Michael, in the hallway outside the bathroom, hangs from a six-foot ladder attached to the wall and says, “Look at this, Charles. This is a special ladder to the roof of The Owl House. Here’s the trapdoor you need to push open if you want to see the enormous fan we use to cool the house.”

Kate looks up at Michael and says, “I love the Third Floor.”

Brenda goes across the hall to her bedroom on the south side and says with pride, “The owl on the top of the roof is perched right above my bedroom.”

There are three latticed windows on the front wall. A large rug on the floor has designs of roses woven into it. Two hickory bureaus with mirrors, one tall and one short, are on opposite sides of the room. A nubby white counterpane covers a four-poster brass bed. The walls have framed architectural blueprints, and prints of Currier and Ives flowers.

Kate plays with the white linen curtains and says, “I love looking out these windows.”

Michael says, “You can see over the lawn and the hedges to Wellington Circle.”

“Wellington Circle is where we play baseball, Charles,” I say.

Dad straightens out one of the finials on Brenda’s bed and says, “Only servants slept in brass beds in the olden days.“

Madelaine, touching a rose on the rug with her foot says, “See the rug? It has roses on it.”

Holly goes out the door and says, “Let's show Charles your home office, Dad.”

We follow her across the hall. Dad’s office has a big square window on one wall. A large oak desk and chair is in front of the window and beside it is an overstuffed file cabinet. The desk has a typewriter on it that is hidden behind piles of books and loose papers. One wall has a floor to ceiling bookcase. There’s a closet filled with boxes of books Dad is supposed to review. Sometimes he needs to cut the pages apart with a small knife.

"Look out this window, Mother, it's really scary. We're so high up," Kate says, "I can see the yellow brick hill."

Madelaine climbs into the big wooden chair behind the desk, "Here's where Dad writes," she says.

Kate squeezes in front of Madelaine to play with the typewriter and says, "This is Dad's typewriter. You can write anything with a typewriter, Charles."

Dad tries to close the overstuffed drawers of the file cabinet. "Look at my poor file cabinet," he says.

I pick up photographs falling out of the bookcase and say, "Dad mostly works at his office at the New Yorker Magazine. He takes a train to Grand Central Station in New York City, Charles."

Holly helps me pick up the photographs. "Dad saved Grand Central Station from being torn down, Charles."

From inside the closet, Brenda says, "Jacqueline Kennedy helped him."

"Tell Charles about Mrs. Kennedy, Dad," says Michael. Charles squeaks.

Dad puts a pile of papers down on his desk and says, "Grand Central Terminal, one of the greatest buildings in America, was in imminent danger of being demolished and, without her help, it surely would have been. Jacqueline Kennedy, despite the fact that she couldn't stand the press, graciously and courageously called me at the Municipal Arts Society, and in her soft voice said, 'I will do anything you ask to help save Grand Central Station.'"

Mother says, "Your father and I rode on a special train from New York to Washington to attract attention to the cause. There were a lot of children on the eight-hour trip. When the children got bored Mrs. Kennedy gathered them together and told them stories about Martin Luther King, and Gandhi, and other great leaders she'd met."

"I love train trips. I never get bored." Kate says.

Holly, with an official voice says, "The tour continues to the guest room."

We go down the hall to the last room on the Third Floor. There are three windows with curtains that match the chintz floral headboards of the twin beds. There's a multi-colored rug between them. A white bureau with a wide scalloped mirror is covered with comic books. There are small bookcases and two closets. Beside the bed, next to the windows, is a large metal box. Inside there's a rope ladder that can be unfurled to reach the sun porch on the floor below in case of fire.

Kate, in front of the windows says, "Look Charles, you can see the sun porch."

Beneath the windows there's an open six-foot by fifteen-foot porch with a high wooden railing.

Madelaine sorts through piles of comics, "Here're all our comic books."

Mother closes a top drawer on the bureau and says, "La commode."

Brenda rearranges the comic books into straight piles and says, "Commode is 'bureau' in English, Charles."

Inside the closet, I open a small door to a narrow hallway where an assortment of canvases painted by Smedley lean against the wall. "Here's our secret closet,

Charles. If you squeeze through this door inside the closet, you go under the roof and over the Gym ceiling," I say.

Michael behind me says, "This closet is a very good place to hide, Charles."

Madelaine, outside the closet says, "You'll never be found, Charles. No one will ever look for you up here."

Holly from the hall says, "The Owl House tour continues to the Second Floor."

Kate tosses a bunch of comic books back on top of the bureau and says, "A bientot Third Floor."

We descend the steep stairs one at a time, bracing ourselves between the banister and walls down to the second floor and our bedrooms.

Chapter 12
The Second Floor

"Two, four, six, eight, who do we appreciate? The Second Floor, The Second Floor, Hurray!"

The second floor has seven bedrooms and four bathrooms.

Holly closes the door to the Third Floor and opens the door to the bathroom beside it. "Here's the first bathroom, Charles," she says.

The bathroom has a Dutch window next to a marble pedestal sink, and a mirrored medicine cabinet above it. A deep porcelain claw foot tub is next to a small toilet.

Michael opens the Dutch window, sticks his head out and says, "See? There's the roof of the porte cochere. We can climb out onto it."

Holly shuts the medicine cabinet and says, "You have to be very careful. Dad climbs onto the porte cochere roof to clean gutters," she says.

"I'm the only one allowed to do that," Dad says.

Mother says, "Pas pour les enfants."

Brenda says, "Pas pour les enfants means 'not for children' in English, Charles."

Kate, in the dry tub says, "Look, Charles, another claw foot tub."

A door leads to a small hall with a cedar closet on one side, and open cupboards on the other leading into Madelaine's bedroom. It has three latticed bay windows over a cushioned window seat, and lavender and green wallpaper. Madelaine sits on her single maple acorn bed covered with a lavender counterpane. "This is my bed," she says.

Brenda, at the end of the bed, looks at a small gold-framed painting of a boy in a straw hat holding an orange and says, "This oil painting looks like you, Charles."

Holly, at the dressing table, fixes her curly hair and says, "I'm the only one in the family with green eyes."

"I have blue eyes," Michael says as he walks by Holly and out the door into the hall.

On the wall of the hall outside Madelaine's room, there's an enormous three-dimensional map of the United States of America.

I reach up to touch it. "Look, Charles, this is a map of America," I say. Charles sighs.

Dad, with his finger, traces a route over the map from New York to California and says, "You can run your fingers over the mountains, ride the great rivers of America."

"O beautiful for spacious skies," Mother sings, and we add our voices to her lyrical soprano and Dad's booming baritone.

Brenda opens a closet door, "Here's our dress up closet," she says.

Inside the closet there are piles of costumes: tri-cornered hats and little silver sabers for pirates, cowboy hats with strings to tie under your chin, holsters and riding chaps, fancy tulle dresses, crowns for princesses, and beaded vests with real moccasins for Indians.

Holly, next to the map, opens another closet door and says, "This is Mother's dress up closet, Charles. These are the fancy clothes Mother wears when she goes with Dad into the city," she says.

The closet is filled with glittering gowns; lovely jet- black satin dresses, organza petticoats, fur- collared jackets, embroidered full skirts, golden lace vests, and a multitude of shiny patent leather high heels.

Madelaine says, "Mother and Dad love to go into New York City, Charles."

Mother says, “Dad and I love to go to New York City. We visit the Metropolitan Museum and the Guggenheim Museum...Frank Lloyd Wright designed the Guggenheim Museum, Children. Frank Lloyd Wright is a friend of Dads. We go to the Whitney Museum and the Pierpont Morgan Library and Lincoln Center..."

“Dad helped start a film festival at Lincoln Center, Charles,” Michael says, And Dad had a play at the Belasco Theatre on Broadway. The play ran for two nights.”

“Two whole nights, Charles,” Madelaine says.

Michael says, “Tell Charles about the play, Dad.”

“Maxwell Anderson and I wrote a play called The Day the Money Stopped. The first line was, ‘I’ve always been so ready to be rich.’ Sadly, the play didn’t succeed and closed after two nights,” Dad says.

“It was a wonderful play, Brendan Michael,” Mother says. Dad laughs.

Michael says, “Time for a tour of my bedroom, Charles.”

In Michael's bedroom there's a row of floor to ceiling leaded windows, a double closet, and a private bathroom with a tall glass shower, toilet and high sink.

"These are my leaded windows, and this is my huge double bed, and my bureau with its big mirror to see my handsome face," Michael says as he kneels on his bed to admire his reflection.

Holly, next to windows says, "Look at the view, Charles." "You can see Wellington Circle again."

I go next door to my bedroom, "Come see my room, everyone," I say.

My bedroom has three large windows that overlook the sun porch. The curtains are embroidered with large multi-colored flowers. There are twin beds with horsehair mattresses covered in bright yellow counterpanes. There's a large mirrored bureau and a small dressing table. The walls have framed color illustrations from Currier and Ives, and one wall is filled with photographs of our ancestors. There's a small closet and a door near one of the beds that leads out to the balcony over the gym.

Kate pulls the balcony door open and says, “Here’s the Gym Charles.”

Madelaine, on a small stool with a tufted top in front of the dressing table mirror says, “Close the balcony door, Kate.”

Dad says, “This is a wonderful room. It’s always filled with light.”

I open a drawer on the sewing table between the beds to get a package of Bazooka bubble gum and give everyone a piece. “Don’t ever chew bubblegum before you go to sleep, Charles. One time I did that and it got all over my p.j.’s, and stuck in my hair,” I say.

Holly pops the gum in her mouth and says, “Charles is too little to chew gum.”

Kate bounces on the bed, “I told you, Charles doesn’t have teeth yet.”

Brenda takes Madelaine's hand and steps down through a door to a narrow bathroom with a window, a modern tub with a shower, and a high sink for grown-ups. “Time for Mother and Dad’s room,” she says.

Kate says, “Dad made all the sinks in The Owl house high up. We have to climb up a step stool to reach our sinks, Charles.”

The master bedroom is painted eggshell white. A high four-poster cherry wood bed is in front of two large windows overlooking Willy’s Garden. On either side of the bed are bookshelves and tables with hand-painted china lamps. In front of the bed is a yellow silk settee. A windowed door next to one of three closets opens to the sun porch. There’s a floor to ceiling mirror on one wall with a wide mahogany bureau and scalloped mirror in front of it. A blue and green Oriental rug covers the floor.

Mother says, “C’est ma chamber, Charles.”

Brenda says, “Chambre is ‘bedroom’ in English, Charles.”

“Can you believe it, Charles? Mother and Dad’s room has three closets!” Michael says.

Holly, on a window seat near the mirrored wall says, “They need them.”

Michael lies on the floor underneath Mother and Dad's bed, "You can sleep here if you want, Charles," he says.

Madelaine, across the room, runs her hands over the blue delft tiles surrounding a small fireplace and says, "These are tiles from Holland. Holland is near France, Charles." She says.

Mother has us spit our gum out into a little wastebasket she's holding, and with a secret smile says, "Brendan Michael..."

Dad turns from examining the top of his bureau and says, "Mother and I have a surprise for the whole Gill family."

Michael, from under the bed says, "Holy cow, another surprise?"

From the sun porch door, Kate says, "Another surprise baby like Charles?"

Dad says, "This surprise is that next summer I've booked passage for the Gill family to travel on the French liner the Flandre. Our ocean voyage will take six days. We'll bring Uncle Charlie's brand new Ford station wagon with modern tubeless tires with us in the hold of the ship. Each of you will have your own trunk to pack and we'll put them on the luggage rack to take wherever we go. The Flandre will dock at Plymouth, England and we'll drive to London to see them change the guard at Buckingham Palace. You'll see the great cathedrals and historic ruins as we go to Stonehenge and Sussex which is in the beautiful English countryside. We'll stay at a little hotel called Park House that is next door to Cowdrey Park, a famous Polo ground. Prince Phillip plays polo there, and Queen Elizabeth often comes to watch him. We'll fly over the English Channel to France. The car will fly with us. We'll visit Paris, and see the Louvre and Notre Dame and the left bank where all the great artists and writers live. We'll be staying at a family hotel right across the street from the Tulleries Gardens. Then, we'll go to Chartres to see its magnificent cathedral. For two nights we'll be staying in the monastery at Mont Saint Michel. We'll need to bring flashlights when we go to the Lascaux caves, where cavemen lived and left evidence of their lives through drawings on the walls. We'll drive to the south of France to St. Jean de Lux where mother lived when she was a child. Then we'll go to the sea at Arcachon, and stay for a week by the lake at Annecy. We'll board the Flandre at Le Harve, France, and six days later return to New York City and our beloved Owl House."

Mother gives Dad a big kiss and says, "C'est extraordinaire, Brendan Michael, Merci Mille Fois."

Brenda says, "Merci Mille Fois, means 'thank you a million times' in English, Charles."

We dance around the bedroom, "Two, four, six, eight," for Dad and Mother, "Hurray!" for London and France and the Flandre, "Hurray! Hurray! Hurray!" and sing, 'Row row row your boat gently down the stream...'

Kate twirls out the door into the hall, and to her bedroom next door. "I want to give Charles a tour of my bedroom now," she says.

Kate's bedroom has two large rectangular windows with a view of the oak tree in Willy's Garden. There's a closet on one wall, and a door to a bathroom on the other. The bathroom has a large window, a claw foot tub and two high up sinks. There is a small step stool hidden in a cabinet under the sink that is easy to pull out and put away. There's a maple sleigh bed with a paisley counterpane, a tall bureau, a small dressing table, and a large woven oval rug. The walls are hung with architectural drawings and handmade pictures. In one corner there's a fancy chair filled with toys.

Kate picks up one of her toys and says, "This is my favorite room to play in, Charles."

Holly steps out into the hall. "The Owl House tour of my room next," she says.

The hall has a banister that looks over the landing on one side, and an ornately framed oil painting from the Renaissance on the wall.

Dad looks at the painting as he walks by and says, "Don't be fooled, this painting is a very good copy."

There's a full-length mirror at the end of the hall. We see Holly with Michael waving his arms behind her and the rest of us behind them.

Kate, up against the mirror, opens her eyes wide and says, "I love the Second Floor."

We crowd into Holly's bedroom. It has windows with views of Willy's Garden and the parapet of the garage. The

Dutch window has a rock pediment below it that is possible to climb down to. There's a small closet next to a mirrored dressing table, and a single maple bed with a green silk counterpane across from an Edwardian bureau and mirror.

Holly opens her Dutch window and says, "Here's my special window. I can look out and wave at everyone who's coming to visit."

Michael flips through Holly's yearbook. "I climbed onto the rock ledge once," he says.

Madelaine, inside Holly's closet says, "I remember that you couldn't climb back in."

Dad says, "Please, children, don't climb out any more windows."

Michael, stepping across the hall to the nursery says, "Let's show Charles his room."

Holly says, "The last room on The Owl House tour."

Charles' room has two latticed windows, one on the south wall, and one on the east. There's a closet next to an Art Deco bureau with a print of a child praying by Currier and Ives on the wall above it. A baby's crib on the opposite wall has a modern poster of an imaginary world above it. Next to the crib is a rocking chair. A large cupboard with shelves is beside the door of the dumb-waiter.

Brenda says, "Look, Charles, you have two windows. One for each side of the house."

Michael, opening the door to the dumbwaiter says, "Here's the dumbwaiter again."

"Madelaine sent Ritz crackers with mayonnaise up in the dumb-waiter when I had the flu," I say.

Madelaine says, "Here's your crib, Charles."

Holly, at the crib says, "Last stop on the tour. It's time for Charles' nap."

"And time for my lovely nap, too," Mother says. Mother takes a nap every day.

Dad says, "I don't know how Mother takes a nap every day. It's remarkable. I've tried to take a naps, but I can't do it. I'm too impatient."

Mother checks the safety pins on Charles' diaper and puts him into his baby sleeping robe. She chirrups at him softly, sits in the rocking chair and sings,

"*Fais dodo, Colas mon p'tit frère*

Fais dodo, t'auras du lolo
Maman est en haut
Qui fait des gâteaux
Papa est en bas
Qui fait du chocolat
Fait dodo Colas mon p'tit frère
Fait dodo, t'auras du lolo."

Everyone listens to her sing Fait dodo to Charles for the first time. She sings Fait dodo to each of us every night. Mother gets up from the rocking chair, kisses Charles on his little hatted head, presents him to each of us to kiss, which we do, puts him in his crib on his stomach and shoos us out of the room.

Kate, with a stage whisper says, "A bientot, Charles." We all start giggling.

"Charles will be up in a minute as soon as he hears the party start," Brenda says.

Mother guides us back down the hall to the top of the stairs and kisses and hugs each of us wherever she can reach, on the top of the head or the cheek, or the neck, and says, "I am so grateful to have such extraordinary children." She smells of Yardley soap and warm milk. Kate holds Mother's beautiful, blue flowered skirt in her hands and says, "A bientot, Mother."

In her beautiful singsong voice, Mother says, "A bientot mes enfants. Je T'aime."

"Je T'aime" "Je T'aime" "Je T'aime" "Je T'aime"

"Je T'aime""Je T'aime" we call out in return.

"It's time to go downstairs to get The Owl House ready for the party," Holly says.

Michael, sliding down the banister says, "I'll make a fire."

Madelaine takes Kate's hand and says, "Kate, you and I can make raisin toast."

"Raisin toast with lots of butter," Kate says.

I go back down the hall to wait outside Charles' door for Dad to reappear. I can hear him singing his lullaby to

Charles, "Believe me if all those endearing young charms that I gaze on so fondly today were to fade by tomorrow and flee from my arms like fairy gifts drifting away, Thou would still be adored as this moment thou art..."

When Dad sings this lullaby to me he sits on the side on my bed and I put my hands in a prayer position and pretend to be asleep. Dad comes out of Charles' room, closes the door gently behind him and sees me. He bends down and offers his cheek for me to kiss. He smells of Old Spice and baby powder.

"Are you waiting for me?" he asks. I nod my head yes. "Thank you, Brenda, I mean Michael, I mean Holly, I mean Madelaine, I mean Kate, and I mean Rosemary... I have so many children I get mixed up," Dad says laughing.

I say, "What's my name, Dad?"

Dad says, "Your name is Rosemary, for remembrance."

We walk down the hall along the carved banister, past the leaded bay windows of the landing, beside the Renaissance oil painting, and I say, "You're funny, Daddy."

Dad looks at me through his horn-rimmed glasses. "I know," he says with a smile.

Dad reminds me of Clark Kent and Superman.

We go downstairs to the chimes of the grandfather clock, under the landing windows and under the arches topped with angels into the front hall that is rapidly filling up with guests. Guests of all ages, shapes, and sizes have come for Charles' first party at The Owl House. "Will we give them a tour of The Owl House, Dad?" I ask. "Of course," he says before the happy flood of friends separates us. When I next hear his voice from the living room "begging silence." That's one of Dad's favorite expressions. When Dad 'begs silence" he is given silence. No one ever wants to miss a word he says, including me. I push my way into the Living Room and join my siblings at his side in front of the fireplace. I look out at the sea of smiling faces and think of the treasures they'll discover at the end of the Owl House tour, Mother and Charles.

Dad raises his glass, "I would like to propose the Gill family toast," he says, "To ourselves, to each other, and to the happiness of us all and to our beloved absent ones, wherever they may be." His glass still raised he says, "And to the newest addition to the Gill family, Charles Barnard Gill who joins Brenda, Michael, Holly, Madelaine, Rosemary and Kate in The Owl House where the first rule of life is to have a good time. There is no second rule." Dad throws his glass into the fireplace, it explodes, as he exclaims, "The Owl House tour will now begin."

"Hear! Hear!" the crowd responds with a thunderous roar and off we go with a "Two, four, six, eight, who do we appreciate. The Owl House, The Owl House, Hurrah!"

Afterword

Brendan Gill

A theme that announces itself again and again throughout history is that of regret for a time that is past. It is said that the oldest specimen of writing that archaeologists have yet discovered bears the message "Too late"-the very message that, several millennia later, the gloomy humorist James Thurber used to scribble on the walls of *The New Yorker* magazine. The implication is always that the past was in some fashion more golden than the present and that the young of any given period have reason to be sorry not to have known the sweetness of life available in their parents' or grandparents' day. And there lies the crux of the matter. For the act of looking back is, by its nature, always an act of falsification, no less strongly felt because it is false; indeed, since the degree to which it is false is usually unconscious, no need to challenge the accuracy of one's recollection is apt to arise. We give our memory credit for an exactitude that it is very far from possessing, and we do so because we must: our very identity is at stake. *Meminisse ergo sum:* I remember, therefore I am. But the fact is that we spend our lives altering our memories, patting them into new shapes and so causing them to come ever closer to our heart's desire. Not how things were, but how we wish them to have been, how we need them to have been, or-to put it more strongly-how we cannot bear for them not to have been is the driving force behind our constant manipulation of the past, whether our own or that of the society in which we have happened (or have chosen) to find ourselves. Eagerly we hold out our hands in greeting our gifted ghosts. We do so with pride and affection, and why should we not? For they are our family, friends and neighbors.

Lawrence Park Bronxville's Turn-Of-The- Century Art Colony 1992

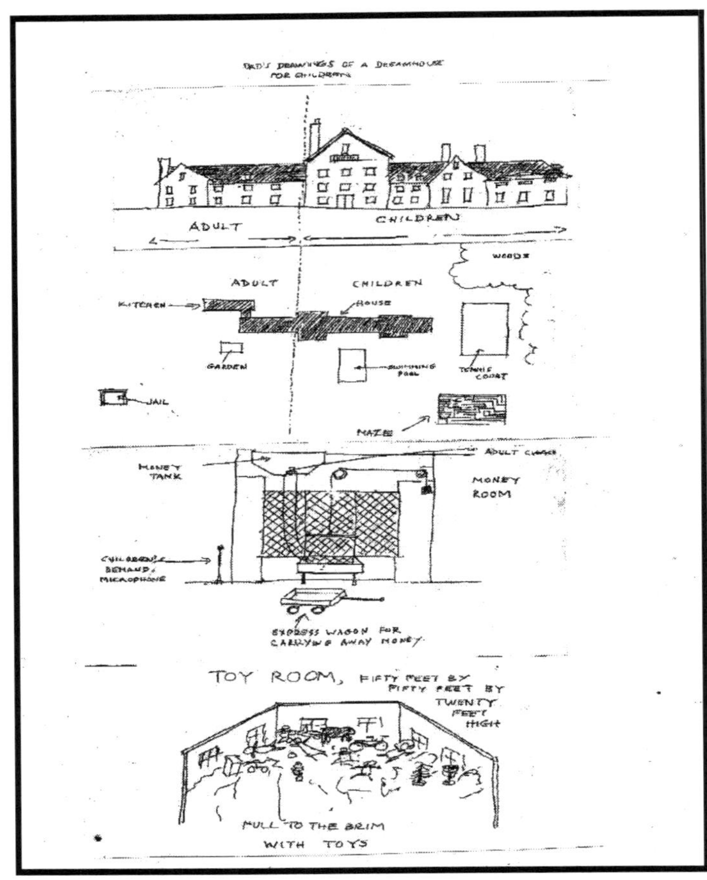

ACKNOWLEDGEMENTS

The Owl House was made possible through the generous support of

Caroline Andrus

Bronxville Historian Eloise Morgan

The Bronxville Public Library

Editor: Susan Levin

Copy Editor: Christine Rhoades

Photos: Bachrach, Roger Haile

ABOUT THE AUTHOR

Rosemary Gill was raised in a wildly creative household. She is an artist, performer and has written four books, ABC"s of the baby 1%, My boss is a baby, Thank you from the bottom of my__________. and When summer stock came to town.

The Owl House, is the true story of growing up in a remarkable family in a remarkable house.

History

The Owl House, originally named "Oak Ridge Cottage," is located at 26 Prescott Avenue, Bronxville, New York. It was built in 1895 and designed by an important architect of the period, William Winthrop Kent. Fellow architect, Arthur Bloodgood Tuttle, wrote in the *Record*, "Oak Ridge...while not the most pretentious in appearance, probably excites interest more than any other house in the park, and more firmly impresses itself on the mind. It is a beautiful structure, irregular and rambling, as it should be, but so well held together, withal, that it may be viewed and judged in its entirety.

The former residence of William T. Smedley, a highly successful portrait painter who vied with John Singer Sargeant for commissions maintained a studio in New York City and two studios at his home in Bronxville. In 1916 Mr. Smedley added a garage which was one of the first to be built in Lawrence Park. Inside he parked a Pierce-Arrow which he never learned to drive.

Lawrence Park Bronxville's turn-of-the-century art colony

Made in the USA
Middletown, DE
15 August 2017